BILINGUAL SONGS

English- French

vol. 1

by
Tracy Ayot
Music by Sa

Produced and P
Sara Jordan Publishing
a division of ℗©2003 Jordan Music Productions Inc.
(SOCAN)

ISBN 1 - 894262-73-5

Acknowledgments

Lyricist - Tracy Ayotte-Irwin
Editor - Marjelaine Caya
Composer and Producer - Sara Jordan
Music Coproducer, Arranger, Engineer - Mark Shannon
Male Singer - Peter LeBuis
Female Singer - Julie Crochetière
Illustrator - pg. 28, 29, 35, 40, 41 - Jessica Jordan-Brough
Digital Illustration Assistant - Ihab El-Shinnawy
Cover Design and Layout - Campbell Creative Services

Digitally Recorded and Mixed by Mark Shannon,
The TreeFort, Toronto, Ontario, 2003.

For further information contact:

Jordan Music Productions Inc.
M.P.O. Box 490
Niagara Falls, NY
U.S.A. 14302-0490

Jordan Music Productions Inc.
Station M, Box 160
Toronto, Ontario
Canada, M6S 4T3

Internet: http://www.sara-jordan.com
e-mail: sjordan@sara-jordan.com
Telephone: 1-800-567-7733

To my dear Tristan, may you always appreciate the richness of our French culture.

À mon cher Tristan, que tu apprécies toujours la richesse de notre culture française.

We acknowledge the financial support of the Government of Canada through the Book Publishing Industry Development Program (BPIDP) for our publishing activities.

We acknowledge the Government of Ontario through the Ontario Media Development Corporation's Ontario Book Initiative.

Contents / Table des matières

Hints for Teachers and Parents

As both a teacher and parent dealing with young people every day, I know how hard it is sometimes to pump excitement and interest into daily classes.

Second language learning research has shown that the use of the first language can aid and enhance the learning of a new language.

The intent of *Bilingual Songs, English-French, vol. 1,* is to liven up second language learning through the rhythm, melodies and exercises here which include both languages.

Second languages need not be strictly used during a certain block of time at school, but can be carried over into many other areas of study (be it music class, gym, drama or creative writing) and, most importantly, go beyond the classroom and become part of students' lives at home and in the community.

Sincerely,

Sara Jordan

President

A few ways to use this resource:

In the classroom:

- ☑ Each song in this volume can be used to teach either French or English.
- ☑ Try lowering the volume of the language being taught to insure active student participation.
- ☑ This resource works well in independent learning resource centers as both a remedial tutorial and as an enriching exercise for advanced students who can write new lyrics using the music accompaniment tracks.
- ☑ As part of a Drama class, have the students act out the various songs. Great fun for "air-band" shows.
- ☑ Encourage students to cover some of the words of their second language (in the book) preferably vocabulary items and try to write them after hearing the song and with the help of their first language.

At home:

- ☑ Whether you listen on the family stereo, through a stereo headset, or in the car as you run errands, *Bilingual Songs, vol 1* can be great fun and entertainment for the entire family.
- ☑ Try singing along using the lyrics book. Maybe you'll discover a star in your own home!

Introduction
Introduction

Hello my friends.
It is time to sing with me.
'Bilingual Songs, Volume 1'
makes learning fun. You will see.

> *Bonjour, mes amis.*
> *C'est le temps de chanter.*
> *Avec «Bilingual Songs, Volume 1»,*
> *c'est plaisant d'apprendre, vous verrez.*

You will be surprised
at how much learning there can be.
What a chance! Sing and dance
with 'Bilingual Songs, Volume 1'.

> *Vous serez surpris*
> *de tout ce que vous aurez appris.*
> *Quelle chance! Chantez, dansez*
> *avec «Bilingual Songs, Volume 1».*

What a chance! Sing and dance
with 'Bilingual Songs, Volume 1'.

> *Quelle chance! Chantez, dansez*
> *avec «Bilingual Songs, Volume 1».*

The Alphabet
L'alphabet

chorus/*refrain* :

The alphabet in French
is easy. You will see!
Let's sing it together
and learn our A, B, Cs.

> *L'alphabet en anglais*
> *c'est facile, tu verras!*
> *Chantons l'alphabet ensemble.*
> *C'est plus facile comme ça.*

A B C D

E F G H

I J K L

M N O P

Q R S T U

V W X Y Z

Je connais mon alphabet.
C'est facile comme tu le sais.

Bilingual Songs - ENGLISH-FRENCH vol.1   ©2003 Sara Jordan Publishing

A B C D
E F G H
I J K L
M N O P
Q R S T U
V W X Y Z

Now I know my A B Cs.
It's so easy. You can see.

Counting to 10
Compter jusqu'à 10

chorus/*refrain 2x :*

I can count.
  Je peux compter.
You can count.
  Tu peux compter.
We can count.
  Nous pouvons compter.
Count!
  Comptez!

One, two, three, four, five,
six, seven, eight, nine, ten.

  Un, deux, trois, quatre, cinq,
  six, sept, huit, neuf, dix.

One, two, three,
Un, deux, trois,

four, five, six,
quatre, cinq, six,

seven, eight,
sept, huit,

nine and ten.
neuf et dix.

One, two, three, four, five,
six, seven, eight, nine, ten.

*Un, deux, trois, quatre, cinq,
six, sept, huit, neuf, dix.*

Days of the Week
Les jours de la semaine

chorus/*refrain 2x :*

Let's sing the days of the week!
> *Chantons les jours de la semaine!*
Let's sing the days of the week!
> *Chantons les jours de la semaine!*

Sunday   *dimanche*

Monday   *lundi*

Tuesday   *mardi*

Wednesday   *mercredi*

Thursday   *jeudi*

Friday   *vendredi*

Saturday   *samedi*

LET'S SING! *CHANTONS!*

chorus/*refrain* :

Sunday	*dimanche*
Monday	*lundi*
Tuesday	*mardi*
Wednesday	*mercredi*
Thursday	*jeudi*
Friday	*vendredi*
Saturday	*samedi*

LET'S SING! *CHANTONS!*

chorus/*refrain* 2x :

Let's sing the days of the week!
Chantons les jours de la semaine!
Let's sing the days of the week!
Chantons les jours de la semaine!

Months of the Year
Les mois de l'année

chorus/*refrain* :

January, February,
March, April, May,
June, July,
August, September,
October, November
and December.

Janvier, février,
mars, avril, mai,
juin, juillet,
août, septembre,
octobre, novembre
et décembre.

Each year has twelve months
but my birhday only happens once.
So my favorite month of all
is the one where my birthday falls.

Chaque année a douze mois,
mais on ne me fête seulement qu'une fois
et le mois que je préfère
est donc celui de mon anniversaire.

chorus/*refrain* :

January, February,
March, April, May,
June, July,
August, September,
October, November
and December.

Janvier, février,
mars, avril, mai,
juin, juillet,
août, septembre,
octobre, novembre
et décembre.

Exercises / Exercices

Join the days with arrows.

Reliez les jours de la semaine.

Monday   mercredi

Friday   samedi

Tuesday   lundi

Sunday   jeudi

Wednesday   vendredi

Saturday   dimanche

Thursday   mardi

Complete. Mark the month of your birthday.

Complétez le calendrier et indiquez le mois de votre anniversaire de naissance.

_____ janvier	February _____	_____ mars
April _____	_____ mai	June _____
_____ juillet	August _____	_____ septembre
October _____	_____ novembre	December _____

Weather and Seasons
Le temps et les saisons

How's the weather? Is it hot?
Quel temps fait-il? Fait-il chaud?
In summer the temperature's hotter.
En été, il fait plus chaud.

How's the weather? Is it cold?
Quel temps fait-il? Fait-il froid?
In winter the temperature's colder.
En hiver, il fait plus froid.

chorus/*refrain :*

Autumn and winter, spring and summer,
we love all the seasons the year has to offer.
L'automne, l'hiver, le printemps et l'été,
nous aimons toutes les saisons de l'année.

How's the weather? Is it mild?
> *Quel temps fait-il? Fait-il doux?*

In springtime the temperature's milder.
> *Au printemps, il fait plus doux.*

How's the weather? Is it windy?
> *Quel temps fait-il? Est-ce qu'il vente?*

In autumn the wind blows stronger.
> *En automne, il vente plus fort.*

chorus/*refrain* :

Autumn and winter, spring and summer,
we love all the seasons the year has to offer.
> *L'automne, l'hiver, le printemps et l'été,*
> *nous aimons toutes les saisons de l'année.*

Colors
Les couleurs

chorus/*refrain* :

I like to eat jelly beans. It's fun!
Which color is your favorite one?

J'aime manger des bonbons sucrés.
Quelle est ta couleur préférée?

Orange, yellow, purple, white,
green, pink, blue; Choose now!

Orange, jaune, violet et blanc,
vert, rose, bleu; choisis maintenant!

I like orange.	J'aime l'orange.
I like yellow.	J'aime le jaune.
I don't like purple.	Je n'aime pas le violet.
I don't like white.	Je n'aime pas le blanc.

I like green.	J'aime le vert.
I like pink.	J'aime le rose.
I don't like blue.	Je n'aime pas le bleu.
How about you?	Et toi?

chorus/*refrain* :

I like to eat jelly beans. It's fun!
Which color is your favorite one?

J'aime manger des bonbons sucrés.
Quelle est ta couleur préférée?

Orange, yellow, purple, white,
green, pink, blue; choose now!

Orange, jaune, violet et blanc,
vert, rose, bleu; choisis maintenant!

Exercises / Exercices

Color and label the colors of the palette.

Coloriez et nommez les couleurs de la palette.

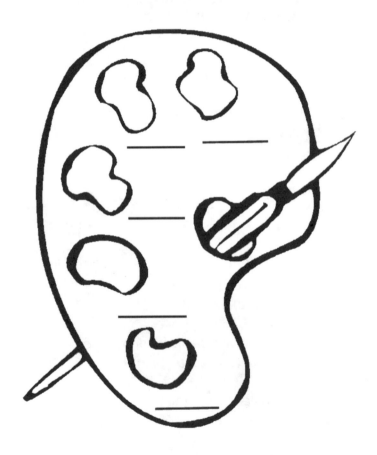

Which colors do you like?

Quelles couleurs aimez-vous?

I like red.	I do not like orange.
J'aime le rouge.	Je n'aime pas l'orange.

_____ | _____

_____ | _____

_____ | _____

_____ | _____

_____ | _____

_____ | _____

Food
La nourriture

chorus/*refrain* :

I feel hungry. Very, very hungry.
I feel hungry. Very, very hungry.
 J'ai faim. J'ai très, très faim.
 J'ai faim. J'ai très, très faim.

We need milk, we need bread.
We need eggs early this morning.
 Il nous faut du lait, il nous faut du pain.
 Il nous faut des oeufs tôt ce matin.

Rice and pasta and some cheese.
Something for the salad if you please.
 Du riz, des pâtes et du fromage,
 et quelque chose pour la salade.

We need orange juice. We need coffee,
soda pop, and we need tea.
> *Il nous faut du jus. Il nous faut du café,*
> *des boissons gazeuses et du thé.*

We need meat and celery.
We need carrots and broccoli.
> *Il nous faut de la viande et du céleri.*
> *Il nous faut des carottes et du brocoli.*

chorus/*refrain* :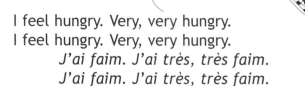

I feel hungry. Very, very hungry.
I feel hungry. Very, very hungry.
> *J'ai faim. J'ai très, très faim.*
> *J'ai faim. J'ai très, très faim.*

Exercise / Exercice

Name the foods.

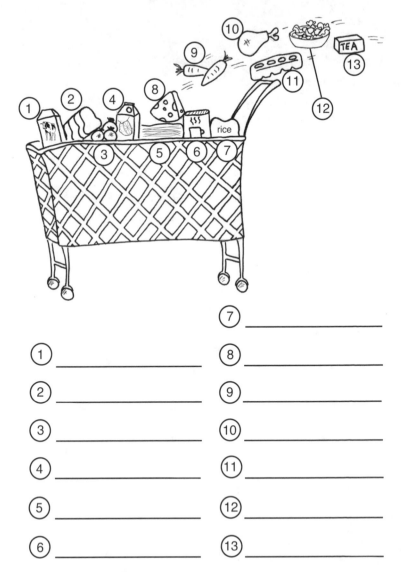

(7) _____

(1) _____

(8) _____

(2) _____

(9) _____

(3) _____

(10) _____

(4) _____

(11) _____

(5) _____

(12) _____

(6) _____

(13) _____

Nommez les aliments.

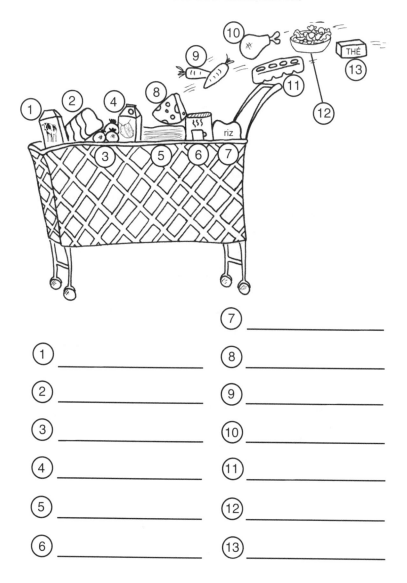

7 _____

1 _____

2 _____

3 _____

4 _____

5 _____

6 _____

8 _____

9 _____

10 _____

11 _____

12 _____

13 _____

The Zoo
Le zoo

chorus/*refrain* :

Do you like going to the zoo?
　　　Aimes-tu aller au zoo?
Let's see all of the animals!
　　　Allons voir tous les animaux!
Lots of things for us to do!
　　　Beaucoup de choses à faire ensemble!
Lots to see at the zoo!
　　　Beaucoup de choses à voir au zoo!

Lions and tigers,
monkeys swinging through the air;
elephants and baboons,
I hope there are animals everywhere!

　　　Des lions et des tigres,
　　　des singes qui se balancent en l'air,
　　　des éléphants et des babouins,
　　　des animaux partout, j'espère.

chorus/*refrain* :

Alligators, crocodiles,
leopards and snakes;
I'm not afraid because
I have got what it takes.

Des alligators, des crocodiles,
des léopards et des serpents
Je n'ai peur de rien,
car je suis confiant(e).

chorus/*refrain* :

Zebras and giraffes,
big gorillas and bears;
lots of animals at the zoo.
Every day I should be there.

Des zèbres et des girafes,
des gros gorilles et des ours;
Il y a beaucoup d'animaux au zoo,
j'aimerais y aller tous les jours.

chorus/*refrain* :

Exercise / Exercice

Name the animals.

Nommez les animaux.

_____

_____

_____

_____

_____

_____

_____   _____

_____   _____

_____   _____

The Body*
Le corps**

sing 2x / *chantez 2x :*

Touch your head.	*Touche ta tête.*
Touch your shoulders.	*Touche tes épaules.*
Touch your feet.	*Touche tes pieds.*
Touch your knees.	*Touche tes genoux.*
Touch your eyes.	*Touche tes yeux.*
Touch your ears.	*Touche tes oreilles.*
Touch your mouth,	*Touche ta bouche.*
nose and cheeks.	*ton nez et tes joues.*

Head, shoulders, feet and knees,
eyes, ears, mouth, nose and cheeks.

Tête, épaules, pieds et genoux,
yeux, oreilles, bouche, nez et joues.

* The entire song is sung twice through.
** Toute la chanson est chantée deux fois.

Exercise / Exercice

Name the parts of the body.

Nommez les parties du corps.

1 _____ 5 _____

2 _____ 6 _____

3 _____ 7 _____

4 _____ 8 _____

Clothing
Les vêtements

chorus/*refrain* :

When I wake up in the morning
I brush my hair,
wash my face and
decide what to wear.

Quand je me lève le matin,
je me brosse les cheveux,
je me lave le visage et
je porte ce que je veux.

I'll wear a skirt.
  Je porterai une jupe.

I'll wear some pants.
  Je porterai un pantalon.

I'll wear some shoes.
  Je porterai des souliers.

I'll wear some socks.
Je porterai des chaussettes.

chorus/*refrain :*

I'll wear a blouse.
Je porterai un chemisier.

I'll wear a shirt.
Je porterai une chemise.

I'll wear a sweater.
Je porterai un chandail.

I'll wear a jacket.
Je porterai un veston.

chorus/*refrain :*

I'll wear a hat.
Je porterai un chapeau.

I'll wear a rain coat.
Je porterai un imperméable.

I'll wear some boots.
Je porterai des bottes.

Are you ready? Let's go!
Êtes-vous prêts? Allons-y!

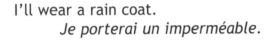

chorus/*refrain :*

Exercise / Exercice

Name the clothing on pages 40 and 41.

Nommez les vêtements des pages 40 et 41.

1) _____

2) _____

3) _____

4) _____

5) _____

6) _____

7) _____

8) _____

9) _____

10) _____

Exercise / Exercice

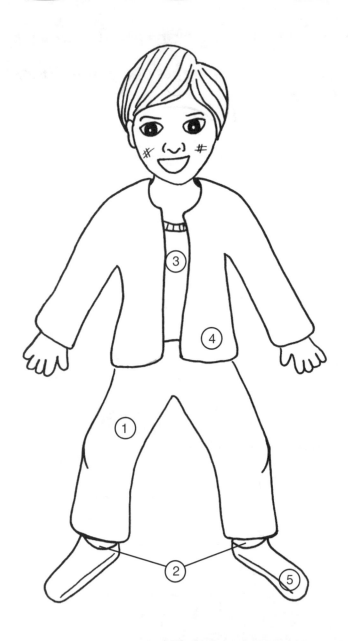

Family
La famille

chorus/*refrain* :

Hi, friend! Let's invite our families
to have a picnic by the lake.
So much food. So many people.
What a great meal we will make.

> *Salut, mon ami! Invitons nos familles,*
> *allons au lac pour un pique-nique.*
> *Tant de nourriture, tant de personnes!*
> *Le repas sera fantastique!*

Let's make a list:
> *Dressons une liste :*

My mother,	*Ma mère,*
father,	*mon père,*
sister,	*ma soeur,*
brother,	*mon frère,*
grandmother,	*ma grand-mère,*
grandfather.	*mon grand-père.*

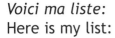

Voici ma liste:
Here is my list:

Ma mère,	My mother,
mon beau-père,	step-father,
mon demi-frère,	step-brother,
mon oncle,	uncle,
ma tante,	aunt,
et mes cousins.	and cousins.

chorus/*refrain* :

Hi, friend! Let's invite our families
to have a picnic by the lake.
So much food. So many people.
What a great meal we will make.

> *Salut, mon ami! Invitons nos familles,*
> *allons au lac pour un pique-nique.*
> *Tant de nourriture, tant de personnes!*
> *Le repas sera fantastique!*

Exercise / Exercice

Name these family members.

Nommez les membres de la famille.

_____   _____

_____   _____   _____

Name these family members.

Nommez les membres de la famille.

_____   _____   _____

_____   _____   _____

Ask your retailer about other excellent audio programs by teacher, Sara Jordan

Bilingual Preschool™

Jump-start learning for preschoolers as they sing and participate in these bilingual songs and games including I Spy, Follow the Leader and Mind Your Manners. This kit teaches: names of animals, counting, directions, polite expressions, places in the community, and counting (cardinal and ordinal numbers). Sung by native speakers, these bilingual songs are a perfect introduction to the new language.
ENGLISH-FRENCH and ENGLISH-SPANISH

Bilingual Songs™ Volumes 1-4

*** Parents' Choice Award Winner! ***

The perfect way to have fun while acquiring a second language. This series teaches the basic alphabet, counting to 100, days of the week, months of the year, colors, food, animals, parts of the body, clothing, family members, emotions, places in the community and the countryside, measurement, opposites, greetings, gender, articles, plural forms of nouns, adjectives, pronouns, adverbs of frequency, question words and much more!
ENGLISH-FRENCH and ENGLISH-SPANISH

Songs and Activities for Early Learners™

Dynamic songs teach the alphabet, counting, parts of the body, members of the family, colors, shapes, fruit and more. Helps students of all ages to learn basic vocabulary easily. The kit includes a lyrics book with activities which teachers may reproduce for their classes.
IN ENGLISH, FRENCH OR SPANISH

Thematic Songs for Learning Language™

Delightful collection of songs and activities teaching salutations, rooms of the house, pets, meals, food and silverware, transportation, communication, parts of the body, clothing, weather and prepositions. Great for ESL classes. The kit includes a lyrics book with activities which teachers may reproduce for their classes.
IN ENGLISH, FRENCH OR SPANISH

Reading Readiness™ Songs

Packaged with a lyrics book which includes helpful hints for parents and teachers. This great introduction to reading uses both phonetic and whole language approaches. Topics covered include the alphabet, vowels, consonants, telling time, days of the week, seasons, the environment and more!
VERSIONS IN ENGLISH, FRENCH OR SPANISH

Grammar Grooves vol. 1™

Ten songs that teach about nouns, pronouns, adjectives, verbs, tenses, adverbs and punctuation. Activities and puzzles, which may be reproduced, are included in the lyrics book to help reinforce learning even further. A complement of music tracks to the 10 songs is included for karaoke performances. Also great for music night productions.
IN ENGLISH, FRENCH OR SPANISH

Funky Phonics®: Learn to Read Volumes 1-4

Blending the best in educational research and practice, Sara Jordan's four part series provides students with the strategies needed to decode words through rhyming, blending and segmenting. Teachers and parents love the lessons while children will find the catchy, toe-tapping tunes fun.
IN ENGLISH

Lullabies Around the World

*** Parents' Choice Award Winner! ***

Traditional lullabies sung by native singers with translated verses in English. Multicultural activities are included in the lyrics book. Includes a complement of music tracks for class performances.
Pre-K - Grade 3 11 DIFFERENT LANGUAGES

The Presidents' Rap®

from Washington to George W. Bush. The legends of the American Presidents live on in classical, swing, dixie, pop and rap music. A musical treasure trove of tid-bits of information on each President. Very popular among teachers wanting to put on musical shows in their school. IN ENGLISH

The Math Unplugged™ Series

Available for Addition, Subtraction, Division and Multiplication. Tuneful songs teach kids the basic math facts. Repetitive, musical and fun. A great resource. Each audio kit includes a lyrics book with worksheet pages which may be reproduced.
IN ENGLISH

Check out these great Resource Books full of reproducible activities and exercises for the classroom.

Bilingual Kids™ Volumes 1-4

Reproducible, black-line, thematic lessons and exercises, based on *Bilingual Songs*, teach the basic alphabet, counting to 100, days of the week, months of the year, colors, food, animals, parts of the body, clothing, family members, emotions, places in the community and the countryside, measurement, opposites, greetings, gender, articles, plural forms of nouns, adjectives, pronouns, adverbs of frequency, question words and much more! ENGLISH-FRENCH and ENGLISH-SPANISH

French for Kids: Beginning Lessons

Reproducible, black-line, thematic lessons and exercises in French, based on *Français pour débutants*, teach the alphabet, numbers, days of the week, opposites, colors, family members, body parts and much more! Lessons are enhanced with information about francophone culture. 64 pages. Beginner level. IN FRENCH

French for Kids: Thematic Lessons

Reproducible, black-line, thematic lessons and exercises in French, based on *Chansons thématiques*, teach common expressions, salutations, time, modes of transportation, pets, prepositions and much more! Lessons are enhanced with information on francophone culture. 64 pages. Beginner level. IN FRENCH

Please visit our English and Spanish websites, great meeting places for kids, teachers and parents on the Internet.

www.SongsThatTeach.com

www.AprendeCantando.com

For help finding a retailer near you contact Sara Jordan Publishing 1-800-567-7733